Investigate

Communities

Neil Morris

Heinemann Library
Chicago, Illinois

www.heinemannraintree.com
Visit our website to find out more information about Heinemann-Raintree books.

To order:
☎ Phone 888-454-2279
💻 Visit www.heinemannraintree.com to browse our catalog and order online.

Edited by Siân Smith, Rebecca Rissman, and Charlotte Guillain
Designed by Joanna Hinton-Malivoire
Original illustrations © Capstone Global Library
Picture research by Elizabeth Alexander and Sally Cole
Originated by Modern Age Repro House Ltd
Printed and bound in China by Leo Paper Group

14 13 12 11 10
10 9 8 7 6 5 4 3 2 1

Library of Congress Cataloging-in-Publication Data
Morris, Neil, 1946-
Communities / Neil Morris.
    p. cm. – (Investigate geography)
  Includes bibliographical references and index.
  ISBN 978-1-4329-3475-0 (hc) – ISBN 978-1-4329-3483-5 (pb) 1.
Communities–Juvenile literature. I. Title.
  HM756.M67 2009
  307–dc22
                        2009011048

Acknowledgments
The author and publishers are grateful to the following for permission to reproduce copyright material: Alamy pp. **4** (© Dennis Frates), **9** (© Imagebroker), **19** (© Wildscape), **23** (© Vario Images GmbH & Co. KG), **24** (© ArkReligion.com); Corbis pp. **8** (© Don Mason), **12** (© Tim Pannell), **14** (© Tim Tadder), **18** (© MM Productions), **25** (© Stuart Freedman), **29** (© Gerry Penny/EPA); Getty Images pp. **6** (Altrendo Images), **10** (Eastphoto/Taxi), **15** (Paul Harris/Stone), **16** (Yellow Dog Productions/The Image Bank), **26** (James P. Blair/National Geographic); iStockphoto pp. **22 bottom**, **22 left**, **22 right**; Photolibrary pp. **5** (Stock 4B/Blend Images), **13** (Kevin Dodge/Flirt Collection), **17** (Image 100), **27** (Shmuel Thaler/Index Stock Imagery), **28** (Corbis).

Cover photograph of Melasti, a Balinese purification ceremony, reproduced with permission of Corbis/© Remi Benali.

Every effort has been made to contact copyright holders of any material reproduced in this book. Any omissions will be rectified in subsequent printings if notice is given to the publisher.

Contents

Some words are shown in bold, **like this**. You can find out what they mean by looking in the glossary.

What Is a Community?

A community is a group of people with something in common. People from different communities may live in the same city or town.

These children may be from the same **neighborhood** or go to the same school.

People form a community by sharing things and doing things together. They live, work, or play together.

6　A person is born into a community. People can also join other communities as they grow up.

One person can belong to a number of communities. You live in a **neighborhood** and go to a particular school. Perhaps you also belong to a club, such as a youth club.

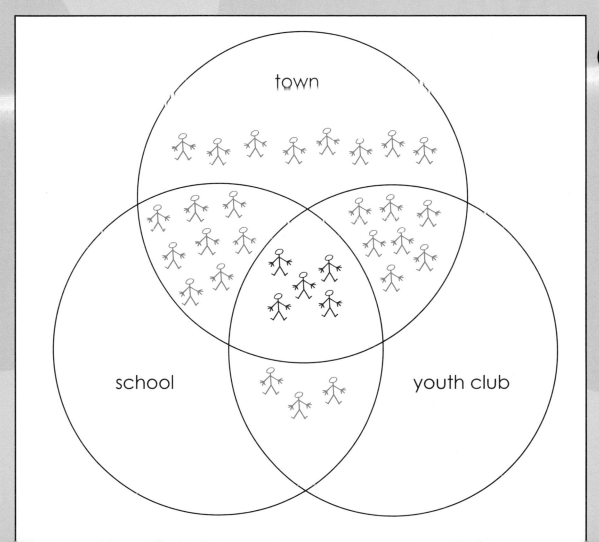

This diagram shows three communities: a town, a school, and a youth club. The people who belong to all three communities are shown in red.

Families

A family can be an important community. Families are usually made up of adults and children. Families can be very different. Some children might live with one parent or two. Some children might live with their grandparents or other people who care for them.

In some countries, people usually have large families. In other countries, parents often have only one or two children.

Q How are you **related** to your mother's father?

CLUE
- Your mother's mother is your grandmother.

9

 **A** Your mother's father is your grandfather.

10

⬆ This man is the girl's grandfather. That means she is his granddaughter.

Some people have **stepparents** or **foster parents**. If a parent marries someone other than the child's birth parent, that person becomes a stepparent. A person who cares for a child in place of the child's birth parents is called a foster parent. We may also have cousins, aunts, and uncles.

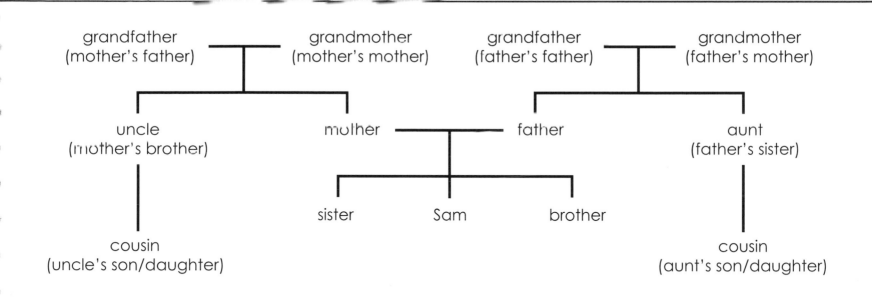

grandfather (mother's father) — grandmother (mother's mother)

grandfather (father's father) — grandmother (father's mother)

uncle (mother's brother)

mother — father

aunt (father's sister)

sister   Sam   brother

cousin (uncle's son/daughter)

cousin (aunt's son/daughter)

 This is a chart of Sam's family. It shows how he is **related** to other people. Sam's aunt, uncle, and cousins do not live in the same place as him.

11

At School

A school is a community of students and teachers. Each grade level also forms its own separate community.

Q

Who is in charge of running a school?

CLUE

- He or she might have his or her own office.

13

 A principal runs a school. He or she is in charge of the other teachers and everyone else who works in the school.

→ Principals have a lot of office work to do. Many also teach in the classroom when they can.

This adult is leading a group of children.

Many different communities have people who act as their leaders. A town has a mayor, and a sports team has a captain.

Friends and Neighbors

Towns and cities are made up of different **districts**. These contain even smaller areas called **neighborhoods**. A neighborhood is a type of community.

↑ People in a neighborhood often see each other every day.

Groups of friends form an important community. Friends do things together that they all enjoy.

Q These friends are also members of a team. Can you guess what they do?

CLUE
- It is a sport.

A

The friends play soccer together.

What other things do you and your friends do together? You may:

➡ play games with toys or on your computer

➡ paint and do crafts

➡ go swimming

➡ do gymnastics or ballet

➡ watch television.

18

People can sometimes go to a local **community center** to meet others. There they can find out about things that are happening in their **neighborhood**.

A community center is a good place to make friends and meet local people.

Communication

People use language to **communicate**. Within most communities people speak a common language. But people can help others by learning and understanding another language.

These are the most-spoken languages in the world.	
Language	**Speakers in millions**
Chinese	873
Spanish	322
English	309
Hindi (spoken in India)	180
Portuguese	177

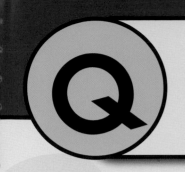 This is how people greet each other in different languages. Do you know which languages they are?

नमस्ते 你好 hola

 CLUES

- They are some of the most-spoken languages in the world.

- Chinese and Hindi use different characters and letters from English.

21

The languages are Hindi, Chinese, and Spanish.

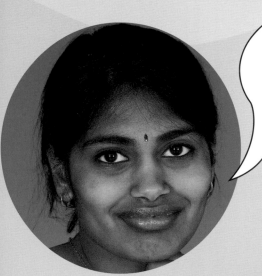

नमस्ते

Hindi

你好

Chinese

hola

Spanish

When people move to another country, they sometimes have to learn a new language. Some young people speak the new language with their community of friends. But they continue speaking the old language with their parents and grandparents.

These adults are learning a new language.

23

Religions

Religious people believe in a faith. The ideas, traditions, and beliefs that they share make them a community.

⬆ These children attend a Christian Sunday school.

Q To which religion does this wedding couple belong?

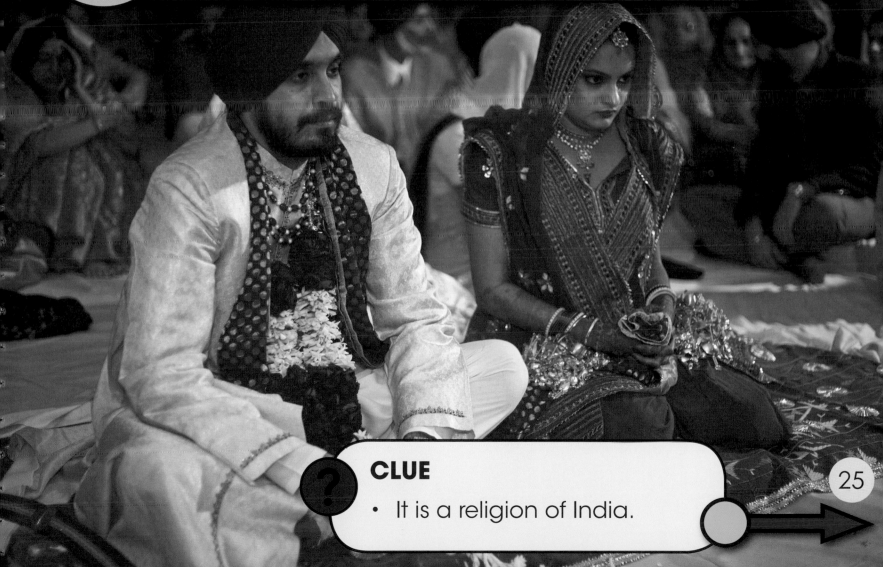

CLUE
- It is a religion of India.

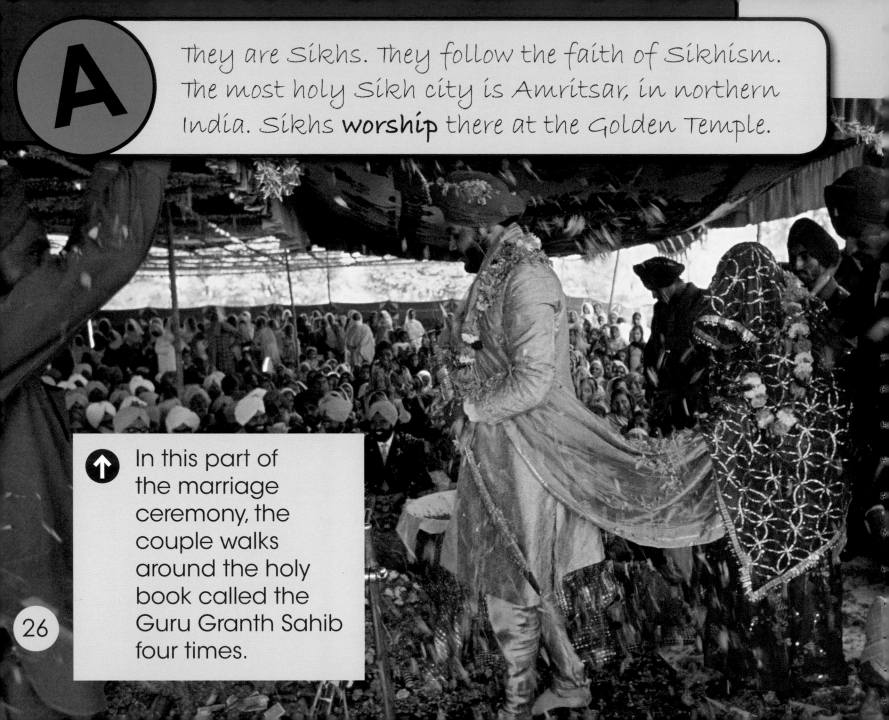

A They are Sikhs. They follow the faith of Sikhism. The most holy Sikh city is Amritsar, in northern India. Sikhs **worship** there at the Golden Temple.

⬆ In this part of the marriage ceremony, the couple walks around the holy book called the Guru Granth Sahib four times.

The world's major religions are:

Religion	Person	Place of worship
Buddhism	Buddhist	temple
Christianity	Christian	church
Hinduism	Hindu	mandir
Islam	Muslim	mosque
Judaism	Jew	synagogue
Sikhism	Sikh	gurdwara

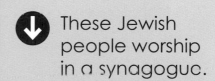 These Jewish people worship in a synagogue.

Understanding Each Other

Being in a community helps us feel that we belong. People in a community often feel special because of the things they have in common with each other.

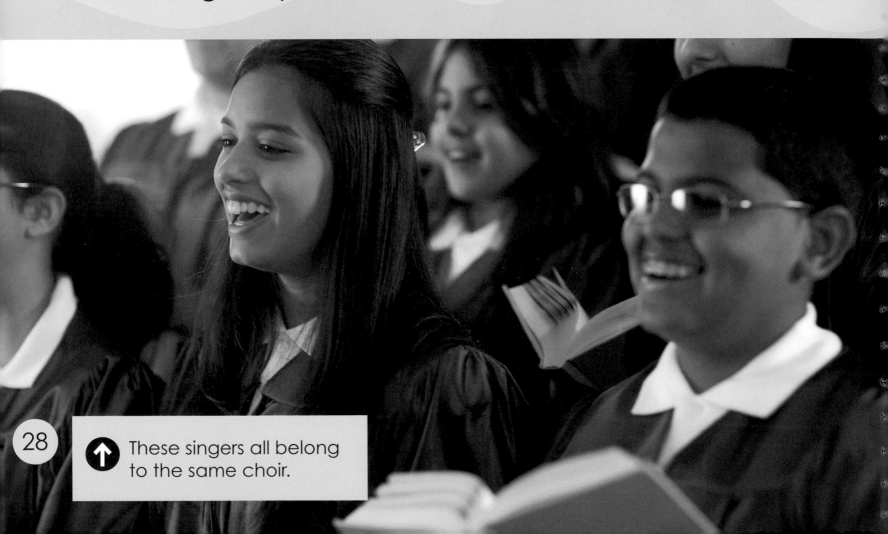

⬆ These singers all belong to the same choir.

↑ These soccer players are members of two different teams. If they all belonged to one team, there would be no soccer match!

We all belong to certain communities. But we must remember that other people belong to different communities from us. They feel special, too.

Checklist

➡ A community is a group of people with something in common.

➡ People form a community by sharing things and doing things together.

➡ People can belong to many different communities.

➡ Families are important communities. There are important communities at school, too.

➡ Friends and neighbors can be important in our lives.

➡ People speak different languages and have different beliefs.

➡ Being in a community helps us feel that we belong. But we must also always respect other people's communities.

Glossary

communicate share information and ideas

community center place where people can meet others in their community and do things together

district area of a town or city (larger than a neighborhood)

foster parent person who cares for a child who is not his or her own by birth

neighborhood local area in a town or city

related to belong to the same family. People who are related are called relatives.

stepparent man or woman who has married a child's mother or father

worship take part in a religious service

Index